# JIU JITSU

## *The Black Belt Syllabus*

### The Official World Jiu Jitsu
### Federation Training Manual

**Professor Robert Clark 9th Dan**

A & C Black · London

First published 1994 by
A & C Black Publishers Ltd
37 Soho Square, London, W1D 3QZ
www.acblack.com

Reprinted 1995, 2000, 2003

ISBN 0 7136 3831 1

A CIP catalogue record for this book
is available from the British Library.

**Acknowledgements**
All photographs by Martin Sellars.
Thanks to Alan Campbell for taking part in the
demonstrations.
Thanks to David Mitchell for helping with
the text.

A & C Black uses paper produced with
elemental chlorine-free pulp, harvested
from managed sustainable forests.

Printed and bound in Great Britain by
The Bath Press, Bath

# Contents

# Foreword

Congratulations on reaching your present standard! You now have a thorough grounding in the basic techniques of jiu jitsu. Once you gain your Black Belt, then you can begin to *learn* techniques. I realise that may sound rather odd, so let me explain. You may think that you have already learned your techniques pretty well, but what you have actually done is to become skilled at copying the instructor. Having reached Black Belt, you will be able to study each technique as it applies to you personally.

As a Black Belt, you will face no more grading examinations cropping up at relatively frequent intervals. This means you no longer have to learn a whole new set of techniques within a short period. The pressure is off, and you can now begin to turn your skill into an art by reviewing and developing all the techniques you have previously practised.

Until now, the effort of concentrating on each part of a throw or hold meant that you performed them mechanically. Now you must aim at performing each technique without conscious thought. This will allow you to look beyond mere execution. Your techniques will become more graceful, powerful, yet seemingly effortless. If the opponent responds in an unexpected way, then you will merely shift gears and slip into an alternative technique. Once, you merely hauled him over regardless. Now you feel his every movement and respond both instinctively and correctly.

Further increase your understanding by showing junior grades how to perform jiu jitsu techniques, because explaining them to others and correcting their errors will give you insights which you could never gain as a student. You may recognise mistakes in students which you failed to pick up in yourself, so through coaching others your own standard will improve. Such is the way of the Black Belt!

So whereas previously you thought of a Black Belt as the ultimate goal to aim for, now you are hopefully coming to realise that it is just the beginning. Be proud of your achievement in coming this far, but now begin to learn the *art* of jiu jitsu.

Robert Clark
*The World Jiu Jitsu Federation*

# The Black Belt Syllabus

## 25 straight throws

The potential Black Belt must be able to perform all the throws learned during the earlier grades. The following throws should have been practised to this point and you may select any 25 for your Black Belt grading.

- Attacking sweeping loin.
- Defending sweeping loin.
- Body drop.
- Dropping version of body drop.
- Dropping version of reverse body drop.
- Crab claw scissors.
- Front scissors throw.
- Hip throw.
- Spring hip throw.
- Inside hock throw.
- Back hock throw.
- Knee wheel.
- Leg wheel.
- Loin or hip wheel.
- Shoulder wheel.
- Outer wheel.
- Leg throw.
- Reclining leg throw.
- Recumbent ankle throw.
- Cross ankle throw.
- Rolling ankle throw.
- Drawing ankle throw.
- Rice bale throw.
- Shoulder throw.
- Full shoulder throw.
- Dropping version of full shoulder throw.
- Half-shoulder throw.
- Arm and shoulder throw.
- Shoulder crash.
- Stamp throw.
- Scooping throw (back and front).
- Valley drop throw.
- Head, hip and knee moves.
- Winding throws (inside and outside).
- Variations on leg sweeps.
- Corner throw.
- Rear throw.

CONTINUED

- Variations on stomach throws.
- Outer hook throw.
- Throwing opponent from behind.

It is not enough merely to perform each throw. You must also follow through with either a strike or a kick, or with a lock or a hold.

I have selected 25 from the above list. The following photographs illustrate the key features of each throw and follow-through. Refer to my two earlier WJJF syllabus books – *White Belt to Green Belt* (A & C Black, 1991) and *Blue Belt to Brown Belt* (A & C Black, 1993) – for full details.

Though I have used certain throws and follow-throughs together, you are not obliged to copy my selection. Simply show you can perform an effective follow-through after each throw, and use as many different follow-throughs as possible.

**Fig. 1** The first throw demonstrated is **body drop**. Draw the opponent forwards so he unbalances over your right leg.

**Fig. 2** Apply a straight arm lever to the opponent's right arm while holding his head down with your left calf.

8

**Fig. 3** The second throw chosen is **half-shoulder**. Straighten your knees and lift the opponent, drawing him forwards at the same time.

**Fig. 4** Kneel on the opponent's mastoid and press down on his extended right elbow. Don't forget to attack the pressure point on the back of his hand!

**Fig. 5** The third technique shown is **leg throw**. Draw the opponent's ankle upwards while pressing against his thigh.

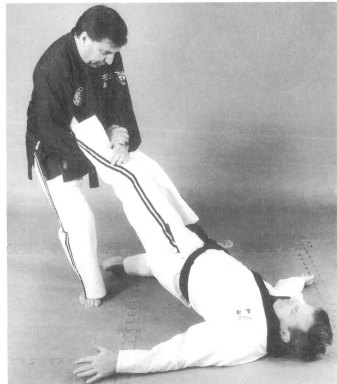

**Fig. 6** Tread on the opponent's right thigh with your left heel and trap his left foot in your right armpit.

**Fig. 7** The fourth throw is **inside hock**. Take the opponent's right wrist and thrust with your right hand-edge while hooking back with your right foot.

**Fig. 8** Perform side kick to the opponent's throat.

**Fig. 9** The fifth throw chosen is **drawing ankle**. Swing your left foot forwards and scoop the opponent's right ankle. At the same time, draw his right arm downwards.

**Fig. 10** Keep hold of the opponent's right arm and draw it out.

**Fig. 11** Turn the opponent onto his front, forcing his right arm up his back. Press down with the flat of your left hand and pin him to the mat.

**Fig. 12** The sixth throw is **attacking sweeping loin**. Swing your right leg back as you draw the opponent across your right hip.

**Fig. 13** Keep hold of the opponent's right arm and follow him down to the mat. Lever his head forwards with your right arm.

**Fig. 14** The seventh throw is **knee wheel**. Lift your right foot as you bring it forwards. Then stamp down on the opponent's knee, push against his left shoulder and draw on his right arm.

**Fig. 15** Follow him down to the mat, then push his right arm to the side and trap it by encircling his neck and shoulder with your right arm. Lower your head and spread your legs wide for stability.

**Fig. 16** The eighth technique is **arm and shoulder throw**. Step to the side to avoid the opponent's right punch, and take his right wrist. Step in, draw his arm up and flex his wrist.

**Fig. 17** Take the opponent face-down to the mat while maintaining your hold on his right arm. Spread your legs wide for good balance and lean forwards.

**Fig. 18** The ninth throw is the **front scissors**. Support yourself on your left elbow and hook your left instep in front of the opponent's right ankle. Then swing your right heel into the back of his knee.

**Fig. 19** Trap the opponent's right foot against your right thigh. Note the position of the guarding hands.

17

**Fig. 20** The tenth throw is a form of the **dropping version of body drop.** Apply leverage to the opponent's right arm as you bar his feet with your left leg.

**Fig. 21** Kneel into the side of the opponent's neck and take his straightened right arm across the front of your thigh.

**Fig. 22** The eleventh throw is the more common **dropping version of body drop.** Drop onto your left knee and bar the opponent's right ankle with your right leg. Draw him forwards by pushing up with your right hand and pulling across with the left.

**Fig. 23** Trap the opponent's head behind your right knee as you pinion his left arm with your right shin. At the same time, apply a lock to the back of his right wrist.

**Fig. 24** The twelfth throw is **scissors** followed by **naked choke hold**. Spin the opponent round and wrap your right forearm across his throat. Note the guarding left hand protecting you from an elbow counter.

**Fig. 25** *Below* Draw the opponent down, sit down behind him and roll back. Hook your ankles together and apply the scissors as you maintain the choke.

**Fig. 26** The thirteenth throw is a **back hock**. Draw the opponent diagonally backwards by pushing with your right hand and drawing with the left. Hook back at his right leg with yours.

**Fig. 27** Trap the opponent's head behind your left knee while locking his right arm straight against your hip.

**Fig. 28** The fourteenth throw is a **front scoop**. Lift the opponent with your right hand as you push back with the left.

**Fig. 29** *Below* Trap his right arm as you encircle his neck with your right arm. Link hands and drop your head low, at the same time spreading your legs wide for greater stability.

**Fig. 30** The fifteenth throw is a **rear scoop**. Drop your right hand onto the back of the opponent's neck and thrust your left hand between his legs. Lift with the left hand and push down with the right hand so the opponent is thrown onto his face.

**Fig. 31** Step quickly through and take up the opponent's arms. Apply a double shoulder dislocation.

**Fig. 32** The sixteenth throw is a **leg wheel**. The opponent takes your belt in his right hand as you force his left arm across his body. Sweep back with your right leg and tumble the opponent forwards.

**Fig. 33** Kneel into the opponent's neck as you fold his right arm over your left forearm. Take your right wrist in your left hand and apply a wristlock.

**Fig. 34** The seventeenth throw is a **double shoulder thrust**. Take the opponent's shins in your hands and jar him forwards with your right shoulder.

**Fig. 35** This photograph is taken from a different angle to show the complexity of the lock chosen. The opponent's head is being levered forwards by your left instep, and his right arm is pinioned behind your right knee. Push his left arm forwards while holding his right in a wristlock.

**Fig. 36** The eighteenth throw uses the **head, hip and knee move**. Sink down on your right knee, drawing the opponent forwards and over your back.

**Fig. 37** *Below* Fold the opponent's right elbow around your left forearm. Thrust your right arm across the opponent's throat, then take your right wrist in your left hand and apply the lock.

**Fig. 38** The nineteenth technique chosen is **rear throw**. Reach for the back of the opponent's neck with your left hand and place your right hand on his stomach. Then sit down and roll back.

**Fig. 39** *Below* Trap the opponent's head behind your right knee as you pinion his left arm with your right instep. At the same time, apply a lock to the back of his right wrist.

**Fig. 40** The twentieth throw is an **outer wind**. Draw the opponent's right arm across your chest and attempt to touch the floor with your right hand.

**Fig. 41** *Below* Bring your right arm behind the opponent's head and trap his right arm with your left foot. Force his head forwards and place the palm of your right hand to the mat just inside his upper left arm. Lean back to apply the lock.

**Fig. 42** The twenty-first throw is the **inner wind**. Thrust your right arm under the opponent's, then try to touch the mat with your right hand.

**Fig. 43** *Below* Keep hold of the opponent's right wrist and draw his arm out straight. Slip your right arm under his and press down against the side of his jaw and throat. Use your own right elbow as the fulcrum, and apply leverage to the opponent's right elbow.

**Fig. 44** The twenty-second throw is the **crab claw scissors**. Drop your right hand to the mat and thrust out your right leg so it passes behind both of the opponent's legs.

**Fig. 45** To make things clearer, this photograph has been taken from the other side. Roll back while hooking your left leg back and into his stomach. Thrust your right arm through his elbow and flex his wrist with your left hand. Take your left wrist in your right hand to apply the lock.

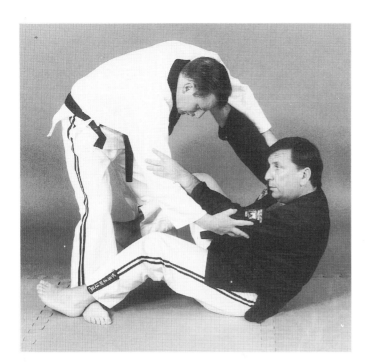

**Fig. 46** The twenty-third technique is a **corner throw**. Step inside the opponent's left ankle with your right foot. Place your left foot to the outside of the opponent's right, and then sit down. This draws him forwards and off balance.

**Fig. 47** *Below* Push your right arm under the opponent's, and step around with your left leg. Fold the opponent's right arm up his back until it is jammed against the front of your right thigh, while your left instep hooks under his chin.

**Fig. 48** The twenty-fourth throw is a **rolling ankle.** Slip your right hand under the opponent's left armpit and step across with your right foot, so it comes to the outside of the opponent's. Sit down and draw the opponent forwards as you bar his right shin with yours.

**Fig. 49** Taken from a different angle, this photograph shows the lock chosen. Step on the opponent's left wrist with your right foot, and lock his right arm against your left forearm.

**Fig. 50** The last of the 25 throws chosen is **spring hip**. Slide your right arm around the opponent's back and draw on his right arm. At the same time, lean forwards and bump his right foot free of the mat.

**Fig. 51** *Below* Follow him down to the mat and apply a straight armlock across your right thigh while pinning his head down with the back of your left knee. Note the position of your left guarding hand.

# Counters to throws

## Half-shoulder throw

**Fig. 52** The opponent steps around and attempts to apply a half-shoulder, but before he can make it work, push his left hip to the side.

**Fig. 53** Then step through with your right foot and take the opponent's right arm with your left hand. Drop to your right knee and draw the opponent over in a head, hip and knee move.

**Fig. 54** *Below* Keep your right arm wrapped around the opponent's neck, and trap his right arm with your right leg.

# Reclining leg throw

**Fig. 55** The opponent drops to one knee and thrusts his right arm behind your knee.

**Fig. 56** *Below* Thrust your left hand forwards as you roll back. This prevents the opponent from attacking your groin or ribs with elbow strike.

**Fig. 57** Quickly bring your left foot forwards and under the opponent's chin, so you can force his head down.

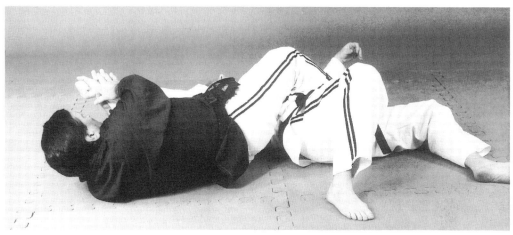

**Fig. 58** *Above* Pull the opponent's right arm straight and lever it over your thigh . . .

**Fig. 59** *Left* . . . then roll over onto your left knee, bringing your left instep across the opponent's throat. The opponent's right arm is trapped behind your left knee and your right shin.

# Outer hook throw

**Fig. 60** The opponent has stepped in and tried to hook your leading left leg with his right leg. At this moment he is less stable than you are.

**Fig. 61** Pull down the opponent's right arm and lift his left. At the same time, withdraw your left foot.

**Fig. 62** Step quickly through with your right leg and hook back into his right leg as you draw him off balance.

**Fig. 63** *Below* Keep hold of his right wrist as he falls, and step over his head with your left foot. Then sit down and lean back, levering his right arm across the front of your thigh.

# Hip throw

**Fig. 64** The opponent slips his right arm around your back and turns to throw you. Press both hands against his right hip to prevent the throw from proceeding.

**Fig. 65** Your left arm entangles his right arm as you thrust your right hand between his legs.

**Fig. 66** Bring your right foot up and roll back. Draw on his right arm and lift with your right hand as you roll him over you.

**Fig. 67** Continue rolling until you come to lie on top of the opponent. Force his right hand behind your right knee. Bring your left forearm across his throat and thrust the right beneath his upper left arm. Then take his wrist in your right hand. Both his arms are now firmly pinioned.

# Shoulder wheel

**Fig. 68** Stop the opponent with your left palm as he dives forwards with his right hand. Now he is in a dangerous position (for him).

**Fig. 69** Keep your guard up as the opponent spins around and tries to punch you with his right fist. At the same time, thrust your right forearm across his chest.

**Fig. 70** Step quickly through with your right foot and swivel your hips. Thrust your right arm under the opponent's elbow and take his wrist. Note your guarding hand.

**Fig. 71** Twist your hips and lean forwards, throwing the opponent to the mat in front of you. Kneel against his mastoid and bring his straightened right arm back and across the front of your right thigh to complete the technique.

# Combination throws

Sometimes your throw does not work as it ought to, and you may be left in a dangerous situation. The following four sequences show how one throw is easily changed into another. Ideally, the second technique must use the opponent's resistance to your first throw in your favour.

## Cross hock into rear throw

**Fig. 72** You attempt cross hock but the opponent thrusts his head forwards and resists.

**Fig. 73** Go with the opponent's resistance and roll back onto the mat. Draw his right arm with your left hand, and lift him by means of your right palm in the pit of his stomach.

**Fig. 74** *Below* Roll with the opponent and force his right hand behind your right knee. Bring your left forearm across his throat and thrust the right beneath his upper left arm. Then take his wrist in your right hand. Both his arms are now firmly pinioned.

# Drawing ankle into sweeping loin

**Fig. 75** Take the opponent's upper arms and attempt to draw him forwards as you bar his right ankle.

**Fig. 76** He pulls back hard, so without changing your hold on him, step through with your right foot and draw him forwards. Sweep his right leg away and throw him.

**Fig. 77** *Below* Keep the opponent's right arm drawn out as you drop to your right knee and thrust your right arm behind his neck. Hook your right hand under his left upper arm, and lever his head forwards. At the same time, force his right arm against your right thigh.

# Half-shoulder into rice bale

**Fig. 78** Step into the opponent, bending your knees and making ready to throw. He sinks his weight and resists.

**Fig. 79** Keeping hold of his right wrist, spin on your left foot and shoot the right foot out. Block his punch with your right forearm.

**Fig. 80** Draw his right arm out to the side as you thrust your right arm past the side of his head. Then loop it around the back of his neck and hook his left upper arm.

CONTINUED

**Fig. 81** Sit down and roll back to perform the throw, then spin round and lock the opponent's right arm while levering his head forwards.

**Fig. 82** This photograph is taken from the other side to show details of the lock used.

# Outer hook into head chancery

**Fig. 83** You attempt an outer hook . . .

**Fig. 84** . . . but your opponent pulls his leg free.

**CONTINUED**

**Fig. 85** Protect your face as you spin around quickly on your left foot and drop your right knee to the mat. Wrap your right arm around the back of the opponent's neck, and trap his left knee with your left arm. Throw him to the mat in front of you.

**Fig. 86** Reach forwards and take the opponent's right lapel in your left hand. Draw the tunic tight across the side of his neck. Press his head forwards and into the choke, using the edge of your right hand.

# Inside leg sweep

**Fig. 87** The opponent attempts to punch you with his right fist. Block him with your right forearm and take his wrist in your left hand.

CONTINUED

**Fig. 88** The opponent next tries to punch with his left fist. Block this too.

**Fig. 89** Attack the opponent's left ear as you spin around on your right foot. Shift weight to your left and swing your right foot forwards.

**Fig. 90** Draw and push the opponent as you hook back with your right leg into his left shin.

**Fig. 91** *Below* Keep a tight grip on the opponent's right wrist, and punch him on the mastoid or temple.

# Defence against kicks

This part of the syllabus requires good timing and correct use of distance. Aim to respond even as the opponent is performing the kick, so that you catch him unprepared. At this point the kick has not yet reached maximum speed, whereas a late response means that you may have to deal with a much faster moving foot!

## Front kick (1)

**Fig. 92** The opponent attempts front kick. Slide forwards on your leading leg and deflect his kick outwards with your left forearm. At the same time, protect your face with your right hand.

**Fig. 93** Thrust your right hand forwards and seize the back of the opponent's neck while hooking at his supporting leg with your right leg. CONTINUED

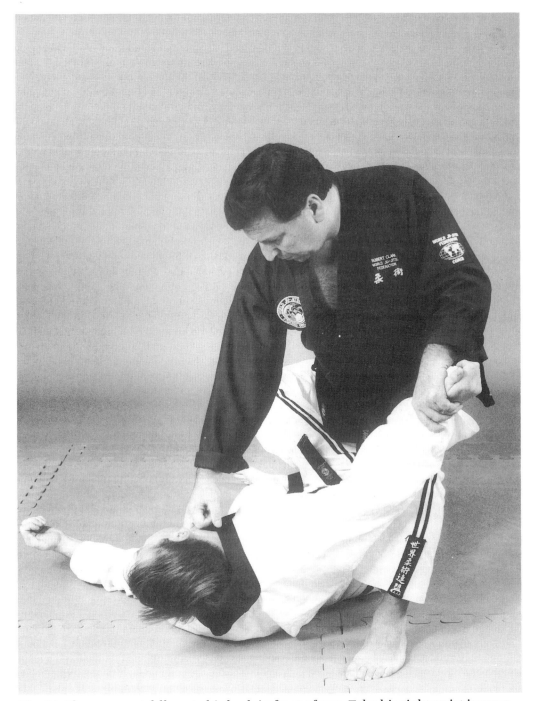

**Fig. 94** The opponent falls onto his back in front of you. Take his right wrist in your left hand and punch him behind the ear.

# Front kick (2)

**Fig. 95** The opponent feints with his right fist to divert your attention.

CONTINUED

**Fig. 96** The opponent attempts front kick but you slide your leading foot forwards, taking his shin between your crossed forearms. Make sure that neither forearm meets the rising shin square-on!

**Fig. 97** Take hold of the opponent's ankle, and both lift and twist it so that he is forced to turn away and fall forwards.

CONTINUED

**Fig. 98** Keep hold of the opponent's ankle, and kick him in the ribs with the ball of your foot.

# Front kick (3)

**Fig. 99** The opponent feints with his right fist. Take it with your left hand and guard your face with the right, swivelling your hips anti-clockwise at the same time.

CONTINUED

**Fig. 100** Keep hold of the opponent's right wrist and deflect his kick with your right forearm.

**Fig. 101** Bring your right forearm up and into the side of the opponent's neck even as he falls backwards.

**Fig. 102** Step through with your right foot and hook it back into the opponent's supporting leg. Draw and push him off balance at the same time.

**Fig. 103** *Below* Drop down onto your right knee and push the opponent's right arm across his body. Then encircle his neck with your right arm and bring your head down close to his.

# Front kick (4)

**Fig. 104** Deflect the opponent's front kick with a sweeping movement of your leading left forearm.

Fig. 105 Turn sharply clockwise behind the block, drawing your trailing right foot around.

Fig. 106 Reach back with your right hand, and take the back of the opponent's collar.

CONTINUED

**Fig. 107** Swing your right foot forwards, then hook it back into the opponent's right leg. This tumbles him backwards and onto the floor at your feet.

**Fig. 108** Bend your knees and punch the opponent just below his ear.

# Roundhouse kick (1)

Roundhouse kick uses a circular action to take the foot into the side of the head or body. Specific counters are necessary to deal with it, and two examples follow.

**Fig. 109** Turn into the kick and bring your right forearm into the kicking shin. Align your block so the opponent's shin strikes near your elbow joint. CONTINUED

**Fig. 110** Your block causes the opponent to drop the spent kick and, in the example shown, he then throws a punch which you block.

**Fig. 111** Block his second punch with your left hand, and seize his upper arm. Lean forwards and thrust your right arm under his left armpit.

**Fig. 112** Slide your right arm around the opponent's back, step around and shoot your right leg out to bar his foot. Draw the opponent forwards and off balance.

**Fig. 113** Bend your knees and strike the opponent's temple with a hammer fist.

# Roundhouse kick (2)

**Fig. 114** In this second example, the opponent attempts a roundhouse kick to your head. Block strongly with your leading forearm.

**Fig. 115** The opponent drops the spent foot and attempts to punch you with his left fist. Deflect the punch outwards.

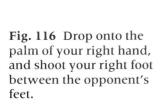

**Fig. 116** Drop onto the palm of your right hand, and shoot your right foot between the opponent's feet.

CONTINUED

**Fig. 117** Hook back with your left heel into the opponent's stomach, and unbalance him backwards.

**Fig. 118** *Below* Complete the throw by raising your left foot high and then dropping it heel-first onto the opponent's breast bone in an axe kick.

# Back kick (1)

**Fig. 119** Step to the side with your leading left foot as the opponent performs back kick. Block his kick with your right forearm. CONTINUED

**Fig. 120** Step forwards with your right foot even before the opponent has a chance to set the spent foot down. Scoop his right thigh with your right forearm.

**Fig. 121** Bring your left foot through, and hook the opponent's left shin as you thrust his upper body forwards with your left hand.

**Fig. 122** Topple the opponent forwards onto the mat, and allow him to begin to roll away from you.

CONTINUED

**Fig. 123** Bring your right foot up and side kick the opponent. Note the left guarding hand.

**Fig. 124** Step right over the opponent with your right foot, and punch him in the groin to complete the sequence.

# Back kick (2)

**Fig. 125** This time, transfer body weight over your rear foot as the opponent performs back kick. Knock his shin outwards with your leading left guard hand.

CONTINUED

**Fig. 126** As the opponent's spent kick falls to the mat, he will be set up ideally to perform a strong punch. Block this with your leading guard hand.

**Fig. 127** Spin around and draw your right foot in. Bend your knees to drop under the opponent's centre of gravity, and stretch his left arm across your left upper arm. Then perform a half-shoulder throw.

**Fig. 128** Keep hold of the opponent's left arm and use your left fist to deliver a punch to his jaw or mastoid.

# Using x-block with knee strike or roundhouse kick

**Fig. 129** The opponent punches with his right fist. Thrust both of your forearms diagonally upwards and forwards, so that they cross in front of your face and trap the opponent's forearm between them.

**Fig. 130** Take the opponent's arm down and to your right. Control his right arm with your right hand.

**Fig. 131** Press the opponent's upper body down and perform knee strike to his face or chest.

**Fig. 132** Set your right foot back down, raise your right fist high above your head and bring your elbow down sharply onto the base of the opponent's skull.

# Using upwards block with throw

**Fig. 133** The opponent throws a punch with his right fist. Thrust your leading left forearm diagonally forwards/upwards, rotating it at the same time so the little finger edge of the fist turns upwards.

**Fig. 134** Take the opponent's right arm down and to the side. As you do so, he punches with his left fist. Turn your hips strongly counter-clockwise, and deflect his second punch with your right forearm.

**Fig. 135** Take the opponent's left arm down and across his body. Keep hold of his right wrist as you do this.

CONTINUED

**Fig. 136** Spin sharply around and step through with your right foot, levering down hard on the opponent's crossed arms. He is forced to rise onto his toes, and he can be thrown easily over your right shoulder.

**Fig. 137** *Below* Follow him down to the mat, pinning his head with your left leg and levering his extended right arm across your right thigh.

# Using the palm heel

Palm heel is a versatile strike used a great deal in jiu jitsu. We covered it in the *Blue Belt to Brown Belt Syllabus* (pages 136 and 137) and here it is again, but this time with more details of its applications.

**Fig. 138** Block the opponent's punch with your left hand, and turn your hips square-on. Transfer body weight forwards, and thrust your right palm heel straight into his jaw.

CONTINUED

**Fig. 139** Turn your hips strongly behind a horizontal circling palm heel that clips the opponent's jaw and rotates his head.

**Fig. 140** Turn your right hip forwards, and deliver right palm heel in an upwards circling swing that clips the opponent's jaw and knocks his head back.

Practise all three basic palm heels in the form of a combination technique.

# Double palm heel strikes

**Fig. 141** The opponent attempts to double punch you. Stop both fists with a double forearm block.

CONTINUED

**Fig. 142** Quickly withdraw both hands to your hips and then thrust them straight back out again, so that they strike either side of the opponent's jaw.

**Fig. 143** This time, use your right palm heel to attack the opponent's jaw, and the left to simultaneously strike his groin.

The jaw and the groin are but two of several targets for palm heel. The following are examples of some other targets.

**Fig. 144** The base of the skull or mastoid are both vulnerable to a palm heel strike.

**Fig. 145** The bridge of the nose makes a good alternative target to the chin.

CONTINUED

**Fig. 146** An upwards blow into the cheek bone is particularly effective.

**Fig. 147** Sink your palm heel deep into the opponent's solar plexus.

**Fig. 148** Strike the opponent's kidneys with double palm heel.

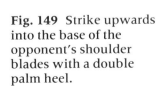

**Fig. 149** Strike upwards into the base of the opponent's shoulder blades with a double palm heel.

CONTINUED

**Fig. 150** Strike the thoracic spine immediately between the shoulder blades with a single palm heel.

**Fig. 151** Use single palm heel to attack the opponent's groin.

**Fig. 152** The joint between the sacrum and the coccyx is also a vulnerable target for palm heel.

**Fig. 153** Drive palm heel into the back of the opponent's knee to collapse his leg.

# Using the open hand

Open hand strikes have been used since the White Belt grade. The purpose of this section of the syllabus is to bring them together and to review them in greater detail.

**Fig. 154** The opponent throws a punch with his right fist, and you block it with your right forearm. Notice the position of your left guarding hand.

**Fig. 155** Continue the hip twist generated by the blocking action, and bring your open right hand behind your left ear.

**Fig. 156** Unwind your hip and cut back into the side of the opponent's neck.

**Fig. 157** Here you have stepped well to the opponent's closed side, deflecting his punch with your right hand. Note the correct foot position.

**Fig. 158** Bring the blocking arm back to your left ear . . .

**Fig. 159** . . . and cut back into the opponent's floating ribs.

**Fig. 160** In this example, begin by transferring body weight to your trailing foot, and block the opponent's punch with your left hand. Draw back your right hand to your ear.

**Fig. 161** Turn your hips strongly towards the opponent, and shift body weight forwards over the leading leg. At the same time, cut to the side of the opponent's neck.

Multiple strikes are required for the Black Belt grading, so study the following and examine how they work.

**Fig. 162** Evade the opponent's punch by twisting your hips and blocking with your right forearm. Take the opponent's wrist in your left hand.

**Fig. 163** Draw the opponent's right arm down and strike back into his neck.

CONTINUED

**Fig. 164** Release the opponent's wrist and wind your hips back, bringing your right hand to the left side of your face.

**Fig. 165** Strike downwards into the opponent's groin.

**Fig. 166** Withdraw your right hand and bring it to the left side of your face once more. Note the position of your left guarding hand.

**Fig. 167** Strike upwards to the base of the nose to complete the sequence.

**Fig. 168** In this next sequence, block the opponent's right fist with your right forearm. Note the well-defined hip twist.

**Fig. 169** Bring your right hand back to the side of your head, and guard with the left.

**Fig. 170** Cut back into the side of the opponent's neck.

**Fig. 171** Counter the opponent's second punch by twisting your hips and blocking with your left forearm.

CONTINUED

**Fig. 172** Cut back with the edge of your left hand into the other side of the opponent's neck.

**Fig. 173** Bring your right hand to the right side of your head.

**Fig. 174** Twist your hips strongly back towards the opponent, draw back your left hand and strike down into the side of his neck to complete the sequence.

107

# Double open hand strikes

**Fig. 175** Block the opponent's right fist with your left forearm, and his left fist with your right forearm.

**Fig. 176** Cross both forearms in front of your chest, turning the little fingers of both fists downwards.

**Fig. 177** Shoot both hands out in a lunging/cutting action which simultaneously strikes both sides of the opponent's neck.

**Fig. 178** Draw back both hands to your ears, as though saluting.

**Fig. 179** Cut with both hands simultaneously to each side of the opponent's neck.

**Fig. 180** Draw back both hands to your hips and transfer weight over the rear foot in preparation for the final strike.

**Fig. 181** Shift body weight forwards and cut to the opponent's floating ribs on both sides with simultaneous, palm-upwards strikes.

111

# Using the elbow

The elbow is a devastating weapon which is at its best in the close-up environment. Make sure you strike with the tip of the elbow and not the length of the forearm, because the former concentrates more power into the strike.

**Fig. 182** Here the elbow is used in an upswinging arc that strikes the opponent under his chin. Note the left hand drawing the opponent's right arm downwards.

112

**Fig. 183** Here the elbow is driven straight back into the opponent's jaw from a half-turned-away position.

**Fig. 184** Draw the opponent's arm down, and twist your hips into him so that your leading foot swivels outwards. Swing your elbow in a horizontal circular strike to the side of his jaw.

**Fig. 185** At first glance, this application looks identical to the previous one, but compare the way in which the two elbows strike their targets. Though this too uses a circular action, here the elbow is travelling *back* into the jaw.

**Fig. 186** Take the opponent's leading arm and step in close, lifting your right fist high above your head.

**Fig. 187** Then drop your elbow downwards onto the opponent's collar bone.

Show how versatile your use of elbow is by incorporating it into a series of techniques such as the following.

**Fig. 188** Deflect the opponent's right fist with an upwards block.

**Fig. 189** Then deflect his left fist with your forearm.

**Fig. 190** Transfer body weight forwards, driving your left elbow back and into the opponent's chest.

**Fig. 191** Spin around on your left foot, and perform a back elbow into the opponent's jaw.

**Fig. 192** In the next sequence, deflect the opponent's right fist with your right forearm, then shift weight forwards and drive your right elbow into his ribs.

**Fig. 193** Turn your back to the opponent and extend your left fist.

118

**Fig. 194** Bring your elbow sharply back and into the opponent's chest.

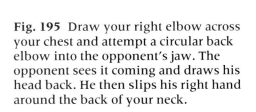

**Fig. 195** Draw your right elbow across your chest and attempt a circular back elbow into the opponent's jaw. The opponent sees it coming and draws his head back. He then slips his right hand around the back of your neck.

**CONTINUED**

**Fig. 196** Trap his right hand and twist anti-clockwise, striking him a second time with your left elbow.

**Fig. 197** Spin clockwise and take the opponent's right arm in a back hammerlock.

**Fig. 198** Raise your right fist as you hold the opponent with the left hand . . .

**Fig. 199** . . . and bring your right elbow sharply down onto the base of the opponent's skull.

# Using the back fist and hammer fist

Back fist is often used in jiu jitsu to distract the opponent so that a lock, hold or throw can be applied. It uses the upper surface of the closed fist in a circular action that is difficult to block.

**Fig. 200** Back fist is useful for attacking the sides of the face and jaw.

**Fig. 201** Back fist can also be used in a vertical strike to the opponent's face.

122

**Fig. 202** Use back fist to attack the opponent's kidney as you step to his closed side.

**Fig. 203** Alternatively, from the same position you can attack the base of his skull.

Step to the side and perform two back fists, one to the kidneys, the other to the head. This will help you to develop the necessary whiplash action.

Practise back fist in a series of moves, such as the following.

**Fig. 204** Use back fist to attack the opponent's groin.

**Fig. 205** Withdraw the groin strike, and use the same right hand to deliver a back fist to the opponent's face.

**Fig. 206** Twist your hips strongly to the right, and wrap your left hand around the back of the opponent's neck.

**Fig. 207** Draw the opponent's head down and complete the sequence with a hammer fist. This application shows clearly the clubbing action used to drop the little finger edge of the closed fist onto the base of the opponent's skull.

Hammer fist is yet another strike which we encountered earlier on. Here, the various applications are brought together into one section.

**Fig. 208** Hammer fist can also be used to attack vertical targets such as the opponent's temple. First block his left fist with your right forearm, then use right hammer fist.

Learn to use a series of hammer fist strikes in a fast and flowing sequence.

**Fig. 209** Block the opponent's left punch with your left forearm. Notice the line you must take up.

126

**Fig. 210** Strike back with left hammer fist into the opponent's ribs.

**Fig. 211** Twist your hips strongly and strike downwards into the opponent's face.

**Fig. 212** In the second sequence, turn your hips strongly and block the opponent's right punch with your right forearm.

**Fig. 213** Quickly raise your right forearm and strike downwards to the opponent's right collar bone.

**Fig. 214** The opponent then punches with his left fist. Turn your hips strongly and block this with your left forearm.

**CONTINUED**

**Fig. 215** Quickly raise your left forearm and strike downwards to the opponent's left collar bone.

**Fig. 216** Twist your hips strongly, raise your right fist and bring it down sharply on the opponent's collar bone.

**Fig. 217** Continue twisting your hips in the same direction and raise your right fist in preparation for the final hammer fist.

**Fig. 218** Use a back-handed action to strike down on the opponent's right collar bone. This concludes the sequence.

131

Hammer fist can be used also as a powerful double block that jams the opponent's punching arm straight.

**Fig. 219** Step to the side as the opponent punches with his right fist. Take his wrist with your right forearm and strike the back of his elbow with a left hammer fist.

**Fig. 220** Take the opponent's trapped arm downwards and . . .

**Fig. 221** . . . strike downwards to the base of his skull with right hammer fist.

Reverse hammer fist uses the thumb side of the rolled fist in either a single or a double action.

**Fig. 222** Curl your left hand around the back of the opponent's head, and draw his head down. Then swing your closed fist up and under his chin, striking with the thumb side.

**Fig. 223** In this example, you have stepped quickly to the side, avoiding the opponent's punch. Take both your arms to the side, with the thumbs pointing inwards.

**Fig. 224** Strike inwards with the thumb side of both fists. Right fist strikes the breast bone and the left fist lands between the shoulder blades, doubling the opponent forwards. Help him lean forwards even more by striking him on the base of his skull with a right hammer fist. CONTINUED

135

**Fig. 225** Then raise both fists high above your head . . .

**Fig. 226** . . . and bring them down sharply, the right striking the base of the opponent's skull, and the left between his shoulder blades.

The last sequence uses circular hammer fist strikes in conjunction with knife hand blocks and straight punches.

**Fig. 227** Turn your hips strongly and block the opponent's right fist with your right forearm.

**Fig. 228** Twist back strongly and deflect the opponent's left fist with an open hand block.

CONTINUED

**Fig. 229** Bring both fists to the sides of your head.

**Fig. 230** Strike down with a double hammer fist to the opponent's collar bones.

**Fig. 231** Draw back both fists, and then thrust them back out in a double punch to either side of the opponent's lower chest.

**Fig. 232** Draw back your left fist strongly, using this action to help power a strong linear punch with your right fist to the opponent's solar plexus.

# Using inside cross block in conjunction with a throw

This sequence makes use of the back fist strike which we recently studied.

**Fig. 233** Block the opponent's right punch with your right forearm. Note the position of your left guarding hand.

**Fig. 234** Draw the opponent's fist down, and strike the side of his jaw with a fast back fist.

**Fig. 235** Reach to take the opponent's left ear in your right hand.

**Fig. 236** Step up with your left foot, and slide the right foot across, so preventing the opponent from stepping forwards. Then draw diagonally down with your left hand and pull with your right hand, so that he is forced to tumble over your right leg.

# One-handed throat throw

This technique relies on a pincer-like grip of the windpipe to control the opponent. Do not squeeze too hard!

**Fig. 237** Catch and deflect the opponent's right fist with your left. Shoot your right hand forwards, and take his windpipe between the thumb and the edge of the index finger.

**Fig. 238** This photograph shows the same movement but from the other side.

**Fig. 239** *Below* Returning to the original perspective, drop onto your right knee and lever the opponent's right arm across your thigh. Maintain your grip on his throat.

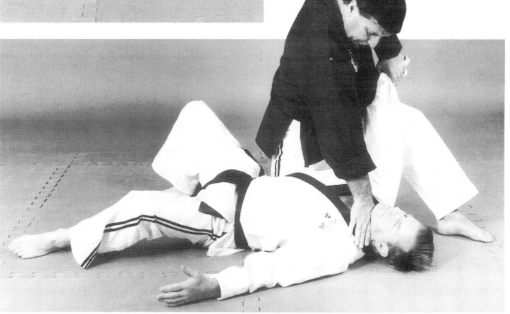

# Attacks to the eyes and ears

These are extremely dangerous techniques which should be practised only under the close supervision of a WJJF qualified instructor. Therefore, I have decided not to describe them in this book.

# Multiple punching

This technique uses a series of straight punches to attack the head and body. You may use both orthodox fists or one-knuckle fists to appropriate targets. The object of practice is to teach you how to rotate your hips fluidly as each punch is launched.

**Fig. 240** Step to the side and counter punch the opponent even as he tries to punch you. Pull the non-punching arm right back to your ribs.

**Fig. 241** Pull back your right fist strongly, using this action plus the hip action to help thrust out your left fist. Extrude the middle joint of the middle finger and strike the opponent in the mastoid.

**Fig. 242** Pull back your left fist and thrust out the right fist in a one-knuckle configuration. This time, strike the opponent's temple.

# Turning, blocking and punching

The object of this training is to help students turn quickly to face and deal with hazards threatening from different angles.

**Fig. 243** *Above left* Deflect the first opponent's punch with a left upwards block.

**Fig. 244** *Above right* Draw back your blocking arm and use this action to help power a reverse punch to the first opponent's mid section.

**Fig. 245** Slide your left foot to the left, withdraw your right fist, and simultaneously perform a second upwards block.

**Fig. 246** *Above left* Withdraw your left fist and perform a second powerful punch.

**Fig. 247** *Above right* Slide your left foot to the left once more, and perform an upwards block to a third opponent.

**Fig. 248** *Right* Withdraw the block and punch with your right fist.

Carry on turning, blocking and punching until you return to the start position. Note that you are always using the left leg as you turn. The upwards block is always made with the left arm, and the punch with the right fist. Then repeat the sequence in the opposite direction, this time leading with the right leg, blocking with the right forearm, and punching with the left fist.

# The kata of blocks

This kata is a training drill intended to help you practise many of the blocks used in jiu jitsu sequentially. The various moves must be performed in the order they are demonstrated here and, more importantly, the advanced student must understand the function and use of each of the blocks demonstrated.

Some blocks use the inside of the forearm, others the outside. The hand edge block concentrates force along a narrow strip and makes for a punishing deflection, while the slightly cupped palm is useful for slapping an opponent's fist to one side.

Many blocks use the leading guard hand to interrupt attacks close to their source – when they are at their weakest – but others function best in a close-range environment. Blocks using the trailing guard hand almost always require a shift in body weight and/or an evasion movement.

Some blocks meet the incoming technique at a right angle and literally slap it out of the air. Others harmonise with a more powerful attack and re-direct it. You must be able to distinguish between all these various types and use the appropriate block for any given situation.

**Fig. 249** *Left* Begin the kata with a formal bow. Place your feet together, close your hands into fists, and incline your head.

**Fig. 250** *Right* Step forwards about a pace-and-a-half with your left leg, and perform a left upwards block. Pull your right fist back to your side.

148

**Fig. 251** *Above* Turn your hips sharply to the right, and wipe your left forearm across your face. The forearm must clear your face in order to be effective.

**Fig. 252** *Above* Now bring your left forearm down in a lower parry that sweeps your mid section free of attack.

**Fig. 253** *Above right* Step forwards with your right foot, and perform right upwards block.

**Fig. 254** Sweep your right forearm across your face and upper body.

CONTINUED

**Fig. 255** *Above* Thrust your right forearm diagonally downwards and outwards in a lower parry.

**Fig. 256** *Above* Step back with your right foot, and perform palm heel block with your left hand.

**Fig. 257** *Above right* Then take a second step back and perform a second palm heel block, this time with your right hand.

**Fig. 258** Step back with your right foot and perform a double block, curling the hands around imaginary attacking techniques.

**Fig. 259** *Above* Step forwards on your right foot and perform a second double block. This time the right hand is high, the left hand low.

**Fig. 260** *Above centre* Step smartly back with the right foot and as you come to a halt, perform a double thrusting palm heel.

**Fig. 261** *Above right* Step up with your trailing right foot and cross your forearms. The right forearm is half extended and held palm down across your chest; the left almost cups your right ear. Look left!

**Fig. 262** Slide your left foot outwards and perform an open hand block with your left hand while leaning away. The right hand is palm upwards on your chest.

CONTINUED

**Fig. 263** *Above* Twist your hips strongly and repeat the open hand block to the right. This time your right hand is extended and the left rests against your chest.

**Fig. 264** *Above right* Turn your hips to the right and draw both hands to your sides.

**Fig. 265** Thrust your right palm out to face height, leaving the left against your rib cage.

**Fig. 266** *Above* Draw your right foot diagonally back, and perform a right open hand thrust.

**Fig. 267** *Above centre* Twist your hips strongly to the right as you draw your right hand back. Sweep your left forearm across your body.

**Fig. 268** *Above right* Step back with your left foot and sweep your right forearm across your body.

**Fig. 269** Draw your right foot back and pull both fists to your hips. Then step out with your left foot and perform a low x-block.

CONTINUED

**Fig. 270** Draw back your left foot, then slide it forwards again, this time performing a high x-block.

**Fig. 271** *Below* Draw back once more, lift your left foot and use it to perform a hooking block against the opponent's front kick. Without once setting the left foot down, complete the sequence with side kick.

**Fig. 272** *Above* Withdraw the spent kick, twist forwards, and step into a left forward stance. Perform elbow block with your left forearm.

**Fig. 273** *Above right* Transfer body weight back, and bring your left forearm downwards.

**Fig. 274** Step diagonally forwards with your right foot, and perform a strong upwards block.

CONTINUED

**Fig. 275** Bring your body weight sharply back, and block downwards with your right forearm.

**Fig. 276** *Below* Draw back your right foot and cross your arms in front of your chest. The right forearm is palm downwards across the chest, the left forearm is raised and the palm turned back towards you.

**Fig. 277** *Right* Continue stepping back with your right foot and perform an open hand block with your leading left hand. Then withdraw your left foot and return to the start position.

# Defence against side snap kick

Side snap kick is a fast version of orthodox side kick. Instead of thrusting the foot edge directly into the target, side snap kick uses a rising action that lacks penetration, yet is effective against such targets as the floating ribs.

**Fig. 278** Take up left fighting stance.

**Fig. 279** Slide your leading left foot to the left, and block downwards with your right forearm.

**CONTINUED**

157

**Fig. 280** *Above* Reach back with your right hand and take the back of the opponent's collar.

**Fig. 281** *Above right* Swing your right foot forwards, then hook it back into the opponent's right leg. This tumbles him backwards and onto the floor at your feet.

**Fig. 282** Bend your knees and punch the opponent just below his ear.

# Further information

Black Belt gradings are held at regular intervals and are always supervised by the WJJF's most senior instructors. Contact your WJJF instructor for full details of grading requirements, or write to:

**The World Jiu Jitsu Federation**
Barlows Lane
Fazakerley
Liverpool L9 9EH

tel: 0151 523 9611

Remember: achieving a Black Belt is a mark of personal skill only – it does not necessarily make you a competent or safe instructor. If you wish to teach other WJJF students, then you must arrange to attend a federation coaching course.

# Index